Helping Children See Jesus

ISBN: 978-1-64104-004-4

Redemption
Set Free From Sin

Old Testament Volume 7:
Exodus Part 2

Author: Arlene Piepgrass
Illustrator: Vernon Henkel
Computer Graphic Artist: Andrew Cross
Typesetting and Layout: Morgan Melton, Patricia Pope

© 2018 Bible Visuals International
PO Box 153, Akron, PA 17501-0153
Phone: (717) 859-1131
www.biblevisuals.org

All rights reserved. No part of this publication may be reproduced, stored in a retrieval system or transmitted in any form by any means, electronic, mechanical, photocopy, recording or otherwise, without the prior permission of the publisher, except as provided by USA copyright law.

RELATED ITEMS

To access related items (such as activities, memory verse posters and translated texts) please visit our web store at www.biblevisuals.org and enter 2007 at the top right of the web page. You may need to reduce the zoom setting to get the search box.

FREE TEXT DOWNLOAD

To obtain a FREE printable copy of the English teaching text (PDF format) under Product Format, please scroll down and select Extra–PDF Teacher Text Download. Then under Language select English before clicking the ADD TO CART button to place in your shopping cart. Other languages are available at an additional cost from the Language menu. When checking out, use coupon code XTACSV17 at checkout and click on Apply Coupon to receive the discount on the English text.

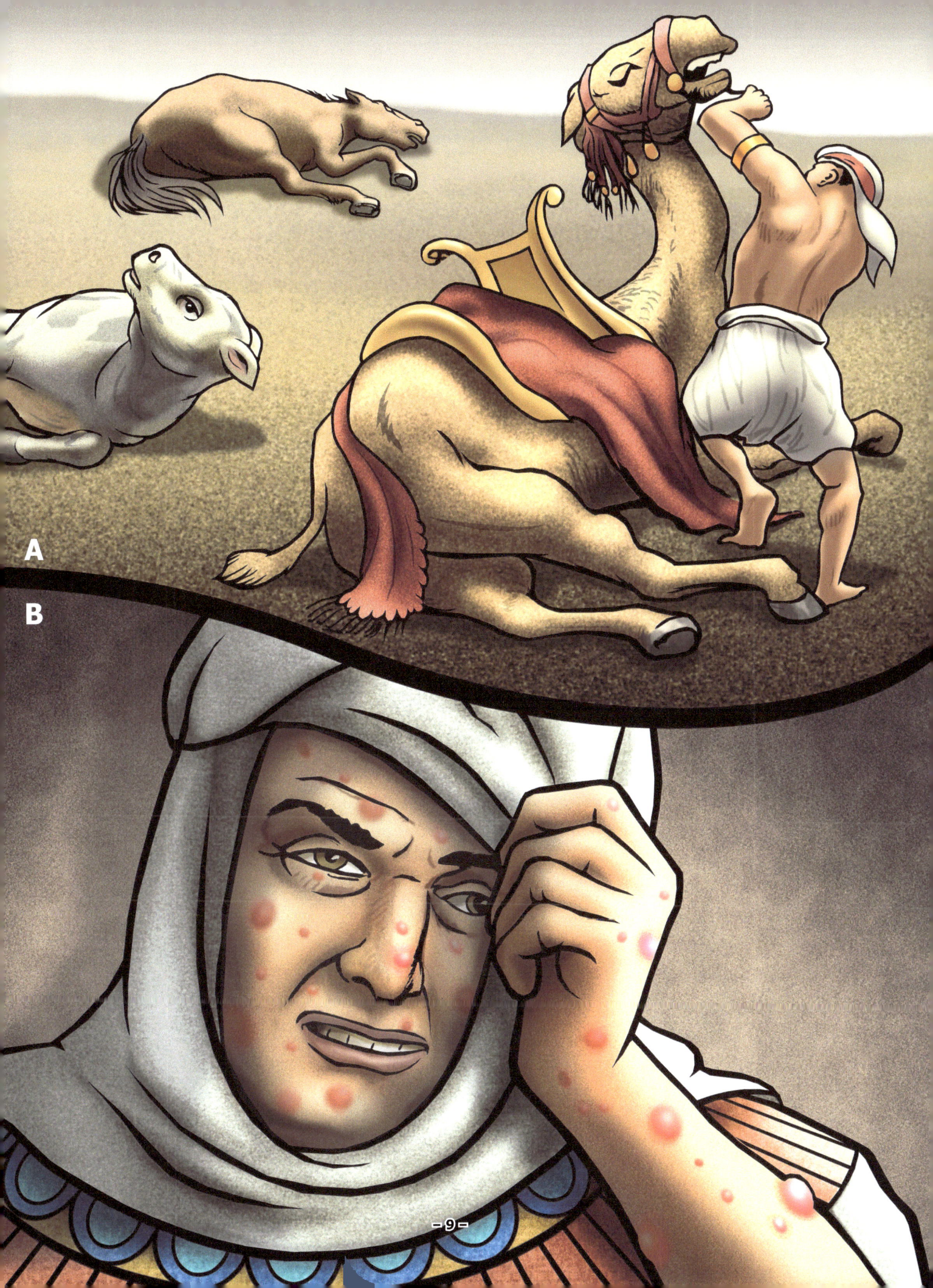

A

B

- 13 -

In Christ we have redemption through His blood, the forgiveness of sins. Ephesians 1:7a

Lesson 1
THE GOD WHO CAN REDEEM

Scripture to be studied: Exodus 4:19-7:25; all verses in the lesson

The *aim* of the lesson: To show that the LORD God is able to set free the slaves of Satan.

What your students should *know*: That the LORD God who, was stronger than Pharaoh, is more powerful than Satan.

What your students should *feel*: Confidence in God and His Word.

What your students should *do*:
  Unsaved: Place their trust in the Lord Jesus Christ for forgiveness of sins.
  Saved: Confess any disobedience to God. Promise to obey Him so He can use them for Himself this week.

Lesson outline (for the teacher's and students' notebooks):
1. God demands obedience (Exodus 4:19-26).
2. God prepares the way ahead (Exodus 4:27-31).
3. God tests faith (Exodus 5:1-23).
4. God is faithful (Exodus 6:1-7:25).

The verse to be memorized:

In [Christ] we have redemption through His blood, the forgiveness of sins. (Ephesians 1:7a)

NOTE TO THE TEACHER

In the book of Exodus we are introduced to the subject of redemption. (See Exodus 6:6.) It is a truth which continues right through the closing book of the Bible. (See Revelation 5:9; 14:3-4.) There is more to this doctrine than is covered in the book of Exodus. Here *redeem* means "to set free by paying a price." It would be well to print this definition on a sign, referring to it often as you teach this series.

In the first two lessons we see the necessity of being set free. In the third lesson we shall see the price paid for redemption. The facts in these lessons (like much Old Testament teaching) illustrate equally important New Testament truths. God's people, the Israelites, were slaves of Pharaoh in Egypt. God bought them back and set them free. These are Old Testament facts. They illustrate the New Testament teaching that we are all slaves to sin. We need to be redeemed. The Lord Jesus Christ, God the Son, paid the price of our freedom when He gave His life on the cross. Help your students to see that Satan clutches his subjects with even greater force than Pharaoh gripped the Israelites.

THE LESSON

Suppose you were the slave of a cruel master. You are under his control day and night. You always have to do what he says. You work like an animal. You can never go anyplace or do anything that you yourself want to go or do. What would you want more than anything else? (*Teacher:* Encourage discussion.)

The people of Israel, whom God had chosen for Himself, were in trouble. Generations of them had lived in Egypt more than 400 years. Now, as slaves to the Egyptians, they were poor, mistreated and overworked. They were not free to choose where to live or what work they would do.

God spoke to Moses from a flaming bush. "I want you to lead My people out of Egypt," He said. "They have suffered long enough. I want them to be free to serve me."

That night Moses talked to his father-in-law, Jethro. "I have been here in this land of Midian a long time [40 years]. I keep wondering about my people in Egypt. Will you let me go back there to see how things are?"

"Yes, certainly, Moses," Jethro replied. "I understand perfectly. Go in peace."

So Moses and his wife packed what they needed for the trip. With their two sons, they began their long journey.

1. GOD DEMANDS OBEDIENCE
Exodus 4:19-26

After a tiring day of travel, Moses and his little family stopped at an inn. During the night, God threatened to kill Moses.

"O God!" Moses prayed. "Did you bring me here to die? Or do You want me to return to Egypt as You said? Do You really want to use me to set my suffering people free from the Egyptians?"

"Yes, Moses, that is exactly what I want you to do," the Lord answered. "But first you must obey Me. You can't lead others unless you yourself are obedient."

Both Moses and his wife understood what God meant. They had disobeyed a command God had given years before. (See Genesis 17:10-14.) That very night they obeyed Him by circumcising their little son.

Show Illustration #1

Now Moses was ready to be used by God. On to Egypt he went, eager to free the Israelite people from slavery.

2. GOD PREPARES THE WAY AHEAD
Exodus 4:27-31

Plodding along, Moses had much time to think. *What will my brother, Aaron, say when I ask him to go with me to the elders of Israel? Will he agree to speak God's words to them?*

At the same time down in Egypt, the Lord spoke to Aaron. "Moses is on his way home," God said. "Go out and meet him."

Show Illustration #2

When they met, the brothers greeted each other warmly. Moses explained, "God knows the awful suffering and slavery of our people. Now He wants to set them free from the Egyptians. He has chosen you and me to be their leaders!"

"Are you sure, Moses?" asked Aaron.

"Yes, Aaron, I am positive," Moses answered. "God did miracles to prove He called us. First my shepherd's rod turned into a snake. Then the snake became a rod. Next my hand turned white with leprosy. Quickly God cured it." (See Exodus 4:3-7.)

– 20 –

After Aaron was convinced, the two brothers went to God's people. The leaders listened when Aaron announced that God would set them free.

"How can we know God has truly spoken to you?" the leaders asked.

Moses threw his rod to the ground and it became a writhing snake. The men jumped back terrified. Moses grabbed it by the tail and it became a rod again. Moses put his hand on his chest inside his robe. When he drew it out, it was white with leprosy. He put his hand inside his robe again. When he brought it out, it was entirely healed.

Moses had another sign to prove that he and Aaron were obeying God. He took water from the river and poured it on dry land. Immediately it turned to blood.

The people exclaimed, "We've seen enough! Truly God has sent you. We'll do whatever you command. We're ready to follow you."

The news spread quickly to all the Israelites: "We won't be slaves any longer! God has called Moses and Aaron to lead us out of Egypt. We'll be free!" The people bowed their heads, thanked God, and worshiped Him.

3. GOD TESTS FAITH
Exodus 5:1-23

Moses and Aaron were afraid as they went to the king of Egypt. But they had a message–and courage–from Almighty God.

Standing before Pharaoh, Aaron spoke with authority. "Your Majesty, we come with a message from the LORD God of Israel. He says His people, the Israelites, are to go to the desert and worship Him."

Show Illustration #3

Pharaoh growled, "The LORD God of Israel! Who is He? I don't know the LORD. And I will NOT let these slaves go anywhere!"

Aaron insisted, "Our God has met with us. We must go for three days and offer sacrifices to Him. If we don't obey Him, we may die."

"Get out of here! Get back to work!" the king demanded. "Quit interfering with the work of my slaves."

Pharaoh dismissed Moses and Aaron and called for his slave masters. "The Israelites want to go–for three days!– to worship their God," he shouted angrily. "From now on, do not give them straw to make bricks. Let them find straw themselves. Make them work harder! But they must make the same number of bricks as before!"

The next day the slaves went all over searching for straw. They worked harder than ever. But at the end of the day, they had made fewer bricks than the day before. The same thing happened the next day.

Show Illustration #4

The slave master shouted, "You didn't make as many bricks! You're not working hard enough. You're lazy! Take that!" he snarled as he lashed the Israelite officers. (See Exodus 5:14.)

Soon the officers, bruised by much beating, went to the king. The speaker began, "Why are you treating us like this? The slave masters won't give us any straw. Yet they insist we make the same number of bricks. This is impossible!" (See Exodus 5:15-16.)

Pharaoh snapped, "Get out of here! Get to work! You are lazy! If you have time to worship the LORD, you have time to find straw!"

Outside, the Israelite officers spoke sharply to Moses and Aaron. "We hope God will judge you for interfering with our business. Pharaoh hates us worse than ever! He's trying to kill us. It's all your fault!" (See Exodus 5:20-21.)

How alone Moses felt! What could he do? No one believed him or listened to him.

Sadly, Moses talked to God. "Lord, why have You treated Your people like this? Things have become much worse for them since I came here. You have not set them free as You promised."

4. GOD IS FAITHFUL
Exodus 6:1-7:25

God did not scold Moses for being discouraged and doubtful. Instead, God spoke tenderly to him.

"Moses, now you will see what I shall do to Pharaoh. I have heard the groaning of My people, the Israelites. (See Exodus 6:5-8.) Tell them I am the LORD God:"

1. "I will redeem them–set them free from slavery." (*Teacher:* Show sign with definition of *redeem*.)
2. "I will take them as My own people."
3. "I will be their God."
4. "I will bring them to their homeland."
5. "I will give them the land of Canaan."

Obediently Moses tried to give God's message to the Israelites. But they refused to listen.

God, knowing all that happened, spoke again. "Moses, go to the palace again. Command Pharaoh to let the children of Israel leave Egypt."

"How can I, LORD?" Moses asked. "My own people, the Israelites, won't listen to me. How can I expect a pagan like Pharaoh to listen." (See Exodus 6:9-13, 28-30.)

"Moses, *I am the LORD*. Do what I say. Leave the rest to Me. When I'm finished, Pharaoh and all the Egyptians are going to know that *I am the LORD*." (See Exodus 6:29-7:5.)

Aaron and Moses obeyed God and went to Pharaoh a second time. "What are you doing here again?" Pharaoh demanded impatiently.

"God sent us to ask you to let all the Israelites leave your country."

"Oh, He did, did He? Prove it!" Pharaoh commanded.

Aaron threw down his rod before Pharaoh. Immediately the rod turned into a snake.

Pharaoh called for his witch doctors who could perform magic tricks. "Do you see what these men have done? Show them you can do the same thing!"

Show Illustration #5

When they threw their rods down, they also turned into snakes. But Aaron's snake swallowed theirs. Still Pharaoh stubbornly refused to let the Israelites leave Egypt. (See Exodus 7:13.)

God then told Moses to meet Pharaoh at the river the next morning. Moses and Aaron obeyed. There they warned

Pharaoh, "The LORD God will show you that *He is the LORD.* If you don't let our people go to the desert to worship Him, all the water will turn to blood."

Show Illustration #6

Pharaoh ignored them and immediately the river turned into blood. The streams, the ponds and pools all turned to blood. The fish died. There was no water for cooking. There was none to drink. For a whole week there was no water–only blood. The odor was sickening. Everyone was miserable!

Pharaoh insisted, "No, you Israelites cannot leave. Get to your work! Stop bothering me!"

Moses did not know *when* or *how* God was going to free the Israelites. But one thing he *did know.* God had said to him, *"I am the LORD.* I am going to redeem you–set you free from the Egyptians." (Show sign defining the word *redeem.*)

Today we are not slaves to a Pharaoh. But all who don't belong to the family of God are slaves of Satan, the enemy of God. He is the toughest of all slave masters. His slaves must obey him every day of their lives. By themselves they can never get free from his clutches.

But God is much more powerful than His enemy, Satan. (See 1 John 4:4.) God sent His Son, the Lord Jesus Christ, who gave His life, His blood on Calvary. Those who place all their trust in Him are set free from their sins. (See 1 Peter 1:18-19.) "In Christ we have redemption through His blood, the forgiveness of sins" (Ephesians 1:7). Are you trusting in Christ alone to forgive your sins and set you free from the power of Satan?

Are you already a child of God? If so, He has work for you to do just as He had work for Moses to do. Like Moses, you must obey God first if you're to be useful to Him. Are you His obedient child? If not, will you confess that disobedience to Him right now? (*Teacher:* Have silent prayer time.) Now will you write in your notebook exactly how you purpose to obey God this week?

Lesson 2
GOD, THE JUDGE

NOTE TO THE TEACHER

From the book of Exodus, we learn four truths regarding the doctrine of redemption:

1. Redemption is entirely from God (Exodus 3:7-8; compare John 3:16).
2. Redemption is through a person (Exodus 3:10; compare John 3:16-17).
3. Redemption is by blood (Exodus 12:13; 23; compare 1 Peter 1:18-19).
4. Redemption is by power (Exodus 6:6; 13:14; compare Romans 3:24; 8:2).

There are opportunities throughout this lesson to emphasize these facts. As often as possible, use your sign defining redeem.

Depending upon the ability of your students, show them that in this section of Exodus God uses His name LORD. LORD (printed in all capital letters) is the name God uses for Himself to tell us He cares about the people whom He created. It is the name He uses in connection with redemption. When sin entered the world, man's sin had to be paid for. It was the LORD God who sought the sinning ones and, by means of a sacrifice, clothed them with coats of skins. (See Genesis 3:9-13, 21.) Throughout all of Scripture, salvation by the LORD is always through the blood of a sacrifice.

Scripture to be studied: Exodus 8:1-11:10; 12:29-36; all verses in the lesson

The *aim* of the lesson: To show that God judges those who disobey Him.

What your students should *know*: That God can protect His own people while judging those who disobey Him.

What your students should *feel*: Amazement that God can be harsh and severe to unbelievers and lovingly kind to believers.

What your students should *do*:
   Unsaved: Accept God's deliverance (redemption) today.
   Saved: Ask the Lord to give them opportunity to witness to unsaved friends this week.

Lesson outline (for the teacher's and students' notebooks):
1. There is no God like the LORD (Exodus 8:1-9:21).
2. God protects those who believe in Him (Exodus 9:22-10:7).
3. What God says is final (Exodus 10:8-29).
4. The judgment of God: death (Exodus 11:1-10).

The verse to be memorized:

In [Christ] we have redemption through His blood, the forgiveness of sins. (Ephesians 1:7a)

THE LESSON

Suppose you make a _____. (*Teacher:* Name something your students might make.) Then accidentally you lost it. Later, seeing it in the hands of another, you ask for it. He replies, "You can't have it unless you buy it. I found it so it's mine." Although it was yours because you made it, you have to buy it back.

So it is with redemption. God made us in His own image for Himself. But because of sin, all of us have lost companionship with God. Now, like all sinners, we are clutched by the enemy of God, Satan. The Lord Jesus, God the Son, gave His life, His precious blood to pay for our sins. When we place all our trust in Him, we're redeemed–bought back by God.

While God's people, the Israelites, were slaves in Egypt they had to obey Pharaoh's commands. God's purpose was to set the Israelites free from Egypt so they could serve the Lord and live for Him. But Pharaoh gripped them tightly for himself.

1. THERE IS NO GOD LIKE THE LORD
Exodus 8:1-9:21

After seven days of having blood only–no water–in Egypt, Pharaoh still refused to release the people of God. So God sent Moses and Aaron back to the palace again. "Our God commands us to go to the desert to worship Him. If you don't give us permission, He'll send a plague of frogs into Egypt."

Pharaoh again refused to let them go. So, at God's command, Aaron held his rod over the water.

Show Illustration #7

Suddenly the whole land of Egypt was covered with cold, slimy frogs. There were frogs in the bread dough and in the ovens. Frogs were in the beds. Frogs were on the tables. Frogs, frogs everywhere!

Because the Egyptians worshiped frogs, they wouldn't kill them. (When people refuse to worship God, they worship all sorts of animals and objects. See Romans 1:21-23.)

When Pharaoh could stand it no longer, he sent for Moses and Aaron. "Pray to your God. Ask Him to take these frogs away. Then I will let your people go to worship the LORD." (See Exodus 8:8-11.)

"When shall I ask God to remove the frogs?" Moses asked.

"Tomorrow," answered Pharaoh.

"All right," replied Moses. "it will be tomorrow. You'll know then that there is none like the LORD our God. He will take away all the frogs except those in the river."

Moses prayed and God answered him. All the frogs died–except those in the river. The people gathered the dead frogs and piled them into heaps. What a smell as they began to rot!

Pharaoh again went back on his promise. He wouldn't let the Israelites leave.

Show Illustration #8A

So God commanded Moses, "Tell Aaron to strike the dust with his rod. I will turn the dust into lice." Immediately all the men, women, children and animals were covered with lice. Everyone scratched all day long.

Standing before Pharaoh his witch-doctors warned him: "This is the finger of God. You're dealing with One who is much greater than our Egyptian gods."

But Pharaoh was too stubborn to listen.

Early the next morning, Moses and Aaron met Pharaoh as he went to the river to bathe.

"What do you two want?" Pharaoh snapped.

"In the name of the living God, let us go to worship the LORD. Unless you do, tomorrow He will send swarms of flies to you and your people. But there will not be one fly where the Israelites live! God will show you that He is the true God. Your false, make-believe gods will not be able to help you. The true and living God will protect us." (See Exodus 8:21-22.)

With that, Moses and Aaron left.

Show Illustration #8B

The next morning, Pharaoh and all the Egyptians were awakened by the buzz, buzz, buzz of flies. (See Exodus 8:24.) Flies swarmed about their heads, covered their food, flew into their mouths, irritated their eyes. But in Goshen, where the Israelites lived, there were no flies–not one!

Pharaoh called Moses saying, "You may worship your God right here in this land."

"That will not do," Moses replied. "If we worship God here, your people will stone us. We must do what God commanded: we must worship Him out in the desert."

Pharaoh answered, "All right. You may go. But hurry! Ask God to destroy these flies!"

Again Moses prayed, God answered and the flies disappeared. With that nuisance gone, Pharaoh again refused to let God's people go.

Moses and Aaron went back to Pharaoh to announce another judgment. "If you refuse to let the Israelites go to worship God, your animals will begin dying tomorrow from a deadly disease. But God will not let any of our animals get sick."

Show Illustration #9A

The next morning Pharaoh learned that the Egyptians' animals were sick. Many were dying. He commanded his servants, "Go see if the Israelites' animals are dying. Let me know immediately."

The Israelites' animals–all of them–were grazing as usual. Not one was sick. Still Pharaoh didn't believe in the true and living God. He refused to let the Israelites go!

Show Illustration #9B

Soon the LORD caused boils to break out on all the Egyptians and on whatever animals were still alive. The people could not work. They moaned and groaned with pain. Even the witch doctors could not stand because of the boils. (See Exodus 9:8-12.) Still Pharaoh refused to let the Israelites go to worship God.

How patient the Lord is! (See 2 Peter 3:9.) Again and again He gave Pharaoh opportunity to repent. But the king became more stubborn and proud.

The next morning, at God's command, Moses went to Pharaoh again. "You have disobeyed Almighty God. Tomorrow He will send the worst hailstorm you have ever seen in Egypt. Warn everyone to bring the remaining animals into the barns. Anything in the fields–animals or people–will be killed." (See Exodus 9:18-21.)

2. GOD PROTECTS THOSE WHO BELIEVE IN HIM
Exodus 9:22-10:7

Show Illustration #10

Exactly as Moses foretold, dark storm clouds gathered over Egypt. Lightning flashed! Thunder rolled! Hail shot down! Fire ran along the ground! And everything in the fields–people, animals, trees–lay dead. God protected the Israelites, however. The storm had not touched them.

Pharaoh was desperate. "Our country will be completely ruined!" he moaned. To Moses and Aaron he admitted, "I have been wrong. Your God is right. Pray to Him. Beg Him to stop this storm. Then you and your people may go."

Moses answered, "I will pray to God. He will stop the storm so you will know He controls the earth. But you had better remember this!"

Moses turned on his heel, walked out of the city, prayed and God answered. The storm passed. Life went back to normal. Alas, Pharaoh again ignored his promise!

Moses and Aaron tramped back to the palace. "How long are you going to be so stubborn? If you refuse to let us go worship God, locusts will cover your whole land tomorrow, so thick that you will not be able to see the ground. They will eat everything that has not been destroyed by hail."

By now the people were angry at Pharaoh. The court officers demanded, "Are you trying to destroy us completely? All Egypt is in ruins. Let the Israelites go serve the LORD their God." (See Exodus 10:7.)

3. WHAT GOD SAYS IS FINAL
Exodus 10:8-29

Pharaoh called for Moses and Aaron. "I have been thinking about your request," he began. "How many of your people will go to worship your God?"

"We are all going," Moses replied. "Our men, wives, children, herds–everybody and everything."

"Never!" Pharaoh exclaimed. "You and your men may go. But leave the rest here in Egypt. Do you understand? Do as I say! Now get out!" (See Exodus 10:11.)

Show Illustration #11A

The next morning, when Pharaoh looked out of his window, locusts covered the earth and hid the sun. They had eaten every green thing. There were locusts, locusts everywhere.

Pharaoh sent for Moses and Aaron. This time he confessed, "I have sinned against the LORD your God and against you. Forgive me. Beg your God to take away these locusts."

Again God answered Moses' prayer. He sent a west wind to carry all the locusts out to the sea. When they were gone, Pharaoh again forbade the Israelites to leave.

Show Illustration #11B

Without warning Pharaoh, God sent darkness–darker than night–over the land of Egypt. It continued all day, all night; all day, all night; all day, all night–three days and three nights. But the Israelites had light as usual!

Calling Moses and Aaron, Pharaoh tried to bargain. "Go worship your God. Take your children with you. But leave your animals here in Egypt." (See Exodus 10:24.)

"No," Moses replied, "we can't leave our animals."

Pharaoh shouted, "Get out of here! If you ever come inside this palace again, you will die!"

4. THE JUDGMENT OF GOD: DEATH
Exodus 11:1-10

Soon, however, Moses returned to Pharaoh with another message from God. "At midnight the LORD will pass through Egypt," he declared. "Your oldest son will die. The oldest son in every home in Egypt will die. Even the firstborn of all your animals will die. Only the Israelites will be spared!" (See Exodus 11:4-6.)

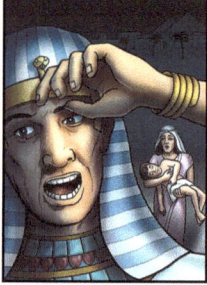
Show Illustration #12

Just as God had warned, at midnight Pharaoh's oldest son collapsed and died. The oldest son of each Egyptian family lay dead. The death wail echoed pitifully from every home. God had done exactly as He said.

A day will come when God will again send judgments to the earth. But what He sends then will be even worse than those He sent to Egypt. (See Matthew 24:21.) The only way to escape God's future judgment is to place your trust in His Son now. Because Christ died on the cross to redeem you, you can be set free from your sins. In Him alone can we "have redemption through His blood, the forgiveness of sins" (Ephesians 1:7). (*Teacher:* Show memory verse.)

If you're already a member of the family of God, you're probably eager to share the Gospel message with unsaved friends. You certainly don't want them to suffer the judgment of God. Will you write in your notebook the name of one to whom you should witness this week? Ask the Lord to show you now how you can approach that person. Together we'll pray that God will prepare him/her to hear His Word from your lips.

Lesson 3
THE PRICE OF REDEMPTION: BLOOD

Scripture to be studied: Exodus 12:1–15:21; Psalms 79, 135, 136

The *aim* of the lesson: To show that we can be redeemed only by the life and blood of Another, God the Son.

  What your students should *know*: That God Himself has provided a Substitute to pay the price of redemption.

  What your students should *feel*: Awed that the perfect Lamb of God paid His blood to set us free from Satan and sin.

  What your students should *do*:
    Unsaved: Place their trust in the Lamb of God for forgiveness of sin.
    Saved: Express praise for their redemption by doing loving deeds for others this week.

Lesson outline (for the teacher's and students' notebooks):

1. The blood of a substitute makes redemption possible (Exodus 12:1-29).
2. The redeemed are removed from slavery (Exodus 12:30-13:16).
3. The redeemed are set free (Exodus 13:17-14:22).
4. God's judgment on the unredeemed (Exodus 14:23-31).
5. The redeemed praise God (Exodus 15:1-21).

The verse to be memorized:

> *In [Christ] we have redemption through His blood, the forgiveness of sins.* (Ephesians 1:7a)

NOTE TO THE TEACHER

Make certain that the doctrine of redemption is perfectly clear to your students. Because the blood of Christ was shed for sinners, those who believe in Him have been purchased, removed from bondage, set free, bought back–this is redemption.

THE LESSON

Fear gripped the hearts of the Egyptians and the Israelites when they heard the tenth terrible announcement which Moses gave Pharaoh. "On the fourteenth day of the month, the firstborn of each family in the land of Egypt will die at midnight." (See Exodus 11:5.)

"*Our* oldest son will die? What can we do to escape?" Everyone was terrified.

The Israelite elders hurried to the meeting which Moses called. They listened carefully to learn God's exact instructions. To make a mistake now would mean death.

1. THE BLOOD OF A SUBSTITUTE MAKES REDEMPTION POSSIBLE
Exodus 12:1-29

The father of each family in Israel was responsible to make everyone understand what they must do and to explain why. Let us listen to a father instructing his son as they stood looking at their flock of sheep.

"Son, today is the tenth of the month. This is the day we must choose a special lamb." (See Exodus 12:3.)

"What kind of lamb do we need, Father?" the son asked as the two looked over the flock.

"First, it must be a male," his father answered. "It cannot be more than a year old. It must be perfect–no defects of any kind. It must be the best of the flock."

Returning to the house the son asked, "What are we going to do with this lamb?"

"We'll keep it here for four days to be certain it's perfect." (See Exodus 12:6.)

The evening of the fourth day, the father instructed, "Son, hold this basin."

"Is this the night, Father?"

"Yes, it is. Tonight the Lord will pass through Egypt. The destroyer will kill the oldest son in every home." (See Exodus 12:23.)

Show Illustration #13A

Quickly his father plunged a knife into the lamb. His son caught the blood in the basin. The father took a bunch of hyssop (a bushy plant) and dipped it into the blood. Carefully he sprinkled the blood above and on each side of the door.

"I won't die, will I, Father?"

"No, you won't. The Lord God will pass over our house–and every house that is sprinkled with blood. God promised, 'When I see the blood, I will pass over you.' (See Exodus 12:13.) Because a lamb has died, you will live."

Inside, the mother was busy following God's commands.

"Mother, you are rushing so, you forgot to put the yeast into the bread dough!" the daughter exclaimed.

"No, my dear, I didn't forget. God said we won't have time for the bread to rise. We're to put the dough in the kneading bowl and wrap it in our clothing so we can carry it with us."

That night all the Israelites dressed for a journey out of Egypt. In their clothing they tied their kneading bowls (filled with bread dough).

Show Illustration #13B

Each family ate its roast lamb without fear–protected by blood on the doorway.

Suddenly, shrill screams of the death wail pierced the midnight silence. Wherever there was no blood around the door, the oldest son lay dead! Even the Crown Prince of Egypt was dead! The firstborn of all the cattle were dead! (See Exodus 12:29.)

2. THE REDEEMED ARE REMOVED FROM SLAVERY
Exodus 12:30-13:16

All the obedient Israelites were alive! The Lord had passed over every home that had blood on the doorposts.

Show Illustration #13

Was it because the Israelites were better than the Egyptians? Was it because the Israelites always obeyed God and lived good lives? Oh, no! This night, all who obeyed God's command were saved by blood. In the same way, you and I cannot be saved from our sin by any good works. We are saved only by trusting in Jesus who shed His blood on the cross for us.

Pharaoh the king called for Moses and Aaron. "Get out of Egypt!" he commanded. "Take your families, your animals–everything–and get out right now!" The Egyptian people also begged the Israelites to leave.

"Yes, yes, we'll go at once," the Israelites agreed. "But please give us some silver, gold and clothing." (God had told them to do this.)

"Here, take all you want!" the Egyptians insisted. "We have lost our oldest sons. Silver and gold mean nothing. Take them! Go, before any more trouble comes to us!"

The Israelites had worked many years with no pay. Now, leaving Egypt, they had much wealth to take with them.

Because of a famine in Canaan, their homeland, 430 years before, 70 Israelites had come to Egypt. During this time many, many children were born. New families had begun.

Show Illustration #14

So now, this night, more than two million Israelites were leaving Egypt!

God told Moses that His people should always remember this event. "Every year in the month of April, the people must celebrate this night," God commanded. "For seven days they must eat bread made without yeast. Each family must kill a lamb, roast it and eat it. This will remind them of the night I killed all the oldest sons in the Egyptians' families. They will recall that their own sons were saved by lamb blood. When your children ask why you're doing these things, explain what happened that night. Then you, your children and your grandchildren will remember that by My strength I redeemed you." (*Teacher:* Show definition. See Exodus 13:3-4, 9, 14, 16.)

This celebration is called the Passover, from God's promise, "I will pass over you."

3. THE REDEEMED ARE SET FREE
Exodus 13:17–14:22

The next morning Pharaoh prepared to bury his son. Every family in Egypt was getting ready for a funeral. What a sad morning for the Egyptians!

For the Israelites it was a happy day. No more brickmaking! No more lashings! They were free!

A large cloud moved before them, directing their march. The Lord Himself was in that cloud, guiding His people. Even at night, He led them, for the cloud became bright as fire, giving them needed light.

When the Egyptian funerals were over, Pharaoh realized he had no one to do any building. There was no one to make bricks. "Why did we let those slaves leave?" the king snorted angrily. "Why did we give them our gold and silver? Get the chariots! Line up the soldiers! We'll overtake those Israelites and bring them back."

Immediately his commands were obeyed. With his army Pharaoh dashed after the Israelites.

The cloud led the Israelites to the shores of the Red Sea. They were surrounded–mountains on one side, a vast desert on the other, water in front of them, Pharaoh and his army pursuing them.

When the Israelites saw the Egyptian chariots, they screamed with terror. "The Egyptians are coming! The Egyptians are coming!" There was no way to escape. They were trapped. They turned to Moses, shouting, "Why did you make us leave Egypt? It was better to be slaves in Egypt than to die out here!"

God ordered Moses, "Tell the people to march forward!" But the Red Sea was in front of them! The sea was deep. They would drown! How could they march forward?

How quickly they forgot all that God had done for them! They forgot that their own sons had lived when the Egyptian sons had been slain.

"Quiet!" Moses commanded. "Stand still! God is going to rescue you! You will never again see the Egyptians. The LORD is going to fight for you!" (See Exodus 14:13-14.)

God continued, "Moses, stretch your rod over the sea."

At that moment the cloud which had been leading them, moved behind them. It was so thick, so low, that the Egyptians couldn't see the Israelites. Nor could they see the way to go. They were forced to stop and wait.

But on the side of the Israelites the cloud became a bright pillar of fire, lighting everything.

Moses stretched his hand over the sea. Suddenly a strong wind blew. The water divided and stood like two high walls. A dry path appeared between the two walls of water.

Show Illustration #15

With dry shoes, more than two million people marched through the Red Sea.

4. GOD'S JUDGMENT ON THE UNREDEEMED
Exodus 14:23-31

The next morning, Pharaoh and his army saw what was happening.

"Mount your horses!" he commanded. "Man your chariots! Get those slaves!"

Pharaoh's army raced into the Red Sea. Suddenly the wheels fell off their chariots. The Egyptians shouted, "Let's get out of here! Quit chasing the Israelites. The LORD is fighting for them! He is against us!" (See Exodus 14:24-25.)

At that moment God commanded, "Moses, stretch your hand over the sea!"

Show Illustration #16

Immediately the walls of water fell with a roar. The Egyptians tried to turn back in the swirling water. But they were too late. Pharaoh, his soldiers and all his horses were drowned! Truly, the Israelites would never see them again. God had redeemed His people. At the price of blood, He bought them back for Himself. They were slaves no longer. God had set them free. And God is the same today. He is the One who redeems us. He sets us free from our enemy, Satan. (See Revelation 5:9.)

How ashamed the Israelites were for the way they had behaved! How embarrassed they were for having spoken against Moses! How patient and long-suffering God is!

5. THE REDEEMED PRAISE GOD
Exodus 15:1-21

Show Illustration #17

Safely on the far side of the Red Sea, the Israelites sang: "The LORD is my strength and song. He is become my salvation. He is my God . . . and I will exalt him . . . O LORD, You in Your mercy have led forth the people which You have redeemed . . . You have guided them in Your strength." (See Exodus 15:2, 13.)

God's instructions for us are as exact and clear as were those for the Israelites. (See John 3:36; 5:24; 1 Peter 1:18-19.) But you do *not* have to kill a lamb and sprinkle its blood about your door. You *do* have to believe that Jesus Christ, God's Son, is the Lamb of God. (See John 1:29.) You must believe He died on the cross of Calvary, giving His blood for your sins. You must understand that when Jesus died, He took your sins upon Himself. He accepted the punishment of death for your sins. Do you believe that the Lamb of God gave His life for you? Will you ask His forgiveness for your sins? Will you receive Him into your heart and life? If so, you will be set free from Satan and his power.

But if you refuse to place your trust in Jesus Christ, God's Son, you will not be redeemed. You will continue to be a slave of Satan and sin.

If you *are* redeemed, you can praise God for your redemption by doing loving deeds for others. List in your notebook kind acts you can do this week which will express your gratitude to the Redeemer.

Lesson 4
REDEMPTION

NOTE TO THE TEACHER

We are introduced to the doctrine of redemption in the book of Exodus. The book of Ruth teaches more about this subject. In the New Testament three thoughts are included in redemption. It means: (1) "to buy or purchase or pay a price," (2) "to purchase out of the market" and (3) "to loose." These ideas are included in the lesson. It would be well to have your students write them in their notebooks along with the simple definition given in the first lesson.

Mention particular sins that chain your students. Help them to see that Satan, who clutches them, allows them to be enslaved by one kind of sin, another and yet another. Usually each sin is increasingly evil.

A person who does not do his best at work may become lazy. Soon he is stealing something most precious: time! What starts in the classroom as cheating may be followed by lying, then stealing. Or anger may finally lead to murder. Smoking tobacco may lead to marijuana, heroin and other drugs. Each sin, like a savage slave-master, binds the sinner more intensely.

Help your students to see that no matter how great may be their slavery in sin, the Lord Jesus is ready, willing and able to redeem them.

Scripture to be studied: Isaiah 14:12-24; 53:5-6; 1 Corinthians 6:19-20; 1 Peter 1:18-19; all verses in the lesson

The *aim* of the lesson: To show the completeness of redemption.

What your students should *know*: The great cost at which Christ purchased us from sin.

What your students should *feel*: Awe that we who chose to sin can be set free to serve the Redeemer.

What your students should *do*:

Unsaved: Place their full and complete trust in God the Son.

Saved: Determine what they can do to show their love for the Saviour.

Lesson outline (for the teacher's and students' notebooks):

1. Redemption needed (Romans 3:10-12, 23; 6:23; Revelation 20:10).
2. Redemption provided (1 Corinthians 6:20; 1 Peter 1:18-19; Revelation 5:9).
3. Redemption accepted (Galatians 3:13; 4:5; Hebrews 9:12).
4. Redeemed sin-slaves become the Lord's servants (Titus 2:14).

The verse to be memorized:

In [Christ] we have redemption through His blood, the forgiveness of sins. (Ephesians 1:7a)

THE LESSON

Try to imagine that you are a Jewish young man living about 2,000 years ago. The great Roman Army recently invaded your homeland and conquered it. And you are a prisoner of war. Now the victorious general is riding into the city of Rome followed by his soldiers. Triumphantly they tramp, tramp, tramp, heads held high, swords gleaming in the sun. Crowds shout and cheer as the treasures roll past: gold, silver, loads of valuables seized from your country.

Suddenly the cheers and shouts change to exclamations of scorn: "Here come the prisoners of war!" "Their uniforms are rags! Ha! Ha!" "Listen to their shuffling feet." "They look like boys, not soldiers." From the corner of your eye you see an important-looking man. He points at you, saying, "That lad looks as if he might be a good slave."

1. REDEMPTION NEEDED
Romans 3:10-12, 23; 6:23; Revelation 20:10

A slave! Your heart races. Your face burns. Your eyes sting. To have been defeated was a disgrace. Being a prisoner may mean torture. But to be a slave! Nothing could be worse.

Show Illustration #4

Slavery is not new. You have heard your parents and grandparents speak about it often. Your people, the Jews, were once slaves in Egypt. How they suffered from the cruel whips of the slave-masters! *Will I be lashed as they were?* you wonder. *I hate these Romans. How can I get free?* You raise your eyes, glancing this way and that. You are chained, surrounded by Roman guards. There is no possible escape. Your head and shoulders sag. You are conquered–owned by another.

After the parade, you and your countrymen are led to the slave market. One after the other is displayed on the slave block. Each is examined by men who buy slaves. You stand there, hands chained, embarrassed, ashamed, confused. You hate the crowds staring at you. You hate the men who inspect you, poking you rudely. You hate their questions. You want to snarl at them, kick them, run away. But you dare not–cannot.

At last the awful day is over. Bound, you shuffle after the man who bought you. You hear him tell another, "I hope this lad will be a good slave. If not, I'll bring him back to the market and sell him to someone else. But if he works well, he'll be mine until he is too old to work. Then I'll sell him for whatever he may be worth."

Now you know the dreadful truth. Never, never again will you be able to do as you want to do. You will not be able to go where you want to go. You are controlled by the one to whom you belong.

Did you know that you and all people born into the world are controlled by another? He is much more powerful, more cruel than any slave owner. He clutches people more stubbornly than Pharaoh held the Jews. Originally his name was Lucifer. He was a beautiful angel created by God. He lived in Heaven right in the presence of God. He served God and worshiped Him. God said he was perfect. (See Ezekiel 28:13-15.)

But a time came when Lucifer decided, "I don't want to worship God. Instead, I want to be worshiped. I shall be like God." (See Isaiah 14:12-14.)

That was sin. And God can't allow sin–certainly not in Heaven. So Lucifer was thrown out of Heaven. His name was changed to Satan, meaning adversary (enemy). Ever since then, Satan has been the enemy of God. He continually tries to spoil all of God's plans. The first man and woman on earth chose to obey him instead of God. Each one born since then has chosen his own way, not God's. (See Isaiah 53:6.) For this reason, all are sinners. (See Romans 3:10-12, 23.) And God says sin must be punished. (See Romans 6:23.)

Some day in the future God will punish Satan and all who listen to him. He will throw them into the lake of fire forever and ever. (See Revelation 20:10.) But God doesn't want *you* to go to that awful place. He wants you to be with Him in His home in Heaven. How can you escape the punishment of sin? How can those who are slaves of Satan be set free from such a powerful enemy? How can sin-slaves be redeemed? (*Teacher:* Show definition.)

2. REDEMPTION PROVIDED
1 Corinthians 6:20; 1 Peter 1:18-19; Revelation 5:9

Show Illustration #13

(When you mention the cross, remove cover from cross on top right of illustration.)

In order to be redeemed, do we need to kill a lamb as the Jewish people did before leaving Egypt? *(No)* Must we eat a Passover meal as they did? *(No)* Are we to sprinkle blood around our door? *(No)* All this was necessary then. But since that time, God the Son has come to earth. Now everything is different. Unlike everyone else, He chose always to do God's will. (See Psalm 40:7-8; Matthew 26:39; John 4:34; 6:38; Hebrews 10:7.) One day He, the perfect, pure sinless Lamb of God took all the punishment for the sins of all. He gave His life on the cross, paying for our sins with His blood. (See Matthew 20:28; Ephesians 1:7; Colossians 1:14; Hebrews 9:22; 1 Peter 1:19; 1 John 1:7; 2:12.) Because God accepted Christ's sacrifice, He arose from the dead and lives forever.

Now, looking down from Heaven, God the Father and God the Son see all people everywhere choosing their own sinful way. Clutched by Satan, controlled by him, people on earth are like slaves in the slave market. Bound by sin, they can't escape.

But wait! The One who created every man, woman, boy and girl is much, much more powerful than Satan, the slave-master. He says, "You and all others, like sheep, have gone astray. You have turned to your own way. But the Lord God has laid all your sin on Me. I am the Lamb of God who takes away the sin of the world." (See Isaiah 53:6; John 1:29; 3:18, 36; 1 Peter 2:24.) Imagine that! He, the perfect Son of God, has paid His blood to redeem you from sin. (See 1 Corinthians 6:19-20; 1 Peter 1:18-19; Revelation 5:9.)

3. REDEMPTION ACCEPTED
Galatians 3:13; 4:5; Hebrews 9:12

It is glorious that the sins of all the world were paid for when Christ died. But there is more. In the time of Moses, each Israelite family had to be inside the blood-sprinkled door for safety. In the same way, each sinner must place all his trust in the Lord Jesus Christ. He does this when he believes that Jesus is the Son of God and asks His forgiveness for sin. Then God removes that person from the sin-slave market, never to be sold again. The true believer is in Christ–a member of the family of God forever. This truth is included in the Bible word *redemption.* (See Galatians 3:13; 4:5; compare John 10:28-29; 17:3, 10-11, 21-22; 1 Peter 1:5.)

It was one thing for the Israelites to believe God and kill a lamb. Every family would do that eagerly, gladly. No one wanted to lose his oldest son. It was quite another matter to believe God and pack up all their belongings and move out of the land of Egypt. But this they had to do if they were to be redeemed–set free from their slavery. They did obey God and miraculously He got them out of the land. Standing on the other shore, the Israelites watched wide-eyed as the Red Sea swallowed the Egyptians.

Show Illustration #17

Immediately they thanked God and praised Him with songs because their slavery was over.

The song they sang is one which any redeemed sin-slave could sing: ". . . The LORD has triumphed gloriously . . . The LORD is my strength . . . He is become my salvation . . . Your right hand, O LORD, is glorious in power: Your right hand, O LORD, has dashed in pieces the enemy . . . You . . . have led forth the people whom You have redeemed . . ." (See Exodus 15:1-21.)

Christ, the perfect One, suffered in our place for our sins and paid for them with His blood. (See 1 Peter 3:18.) When all our trust is in Him, He takes us out of the sin-slave market, never again to be sold as slaves of sin. This is redemption. But there is more.

Again, think of yourself on display in the slave market. One after another examines you to see if you are the kind of slave he wants. Some want slaves with strong arms. Others want those with muscular legs. But one comes along who looks only at your eyes. "I have already paid for you," He whispers. "I buy slaves because I love them and love to buy them. If you will trust completely in Me, you will never, never again be in this slave market. In addition, I will set you free forever. By trusting in Me you will be redeemed." (*Teacher:* Show sign defining redeemed.)

If you were on the slave block, would you trust Him? (Allow class discussion.) Would you do anything for Him?

Years and years ago, the Lord Jesus Christ gave His blood, His life to pay for your sins. But you will continue to be a slave of sin until you place all your trust in Him. Once you do this, you are no longer a sin-slave. Indeed, He who loves you will set you free forever. (See 1 Timothy 2:6; Hebrews 9:12.)

4. REDEEMED SIN-SLAVES BECOME THE LORD'S SERVANTS
Titus 2:14

Are you among the redeemed? If so, you are owned by Another, the Lord Jesus Christ. You are His because He bought you, redeemed you from all sin, and set you free. Now He expects you to serve Him–to do good works for Him. (See Titus 2:14; 3:8.) While He was here on earth, He did the work of a servant. (See Mark 10:43-45; John 13:1-17.) Today, He who is our Lord in Heaven, expects us to take His place, serving others. (See Romans 6:17-18; 2 Corinthians 4:5.)

What does He want you to do for Him? For one thing, He wants you to tell others about Him. They should hear from your lips that He has paid the price for their sins and is waiting to redeem them. Most people don't like to think of themselves as sinners. They may tell you they are really quite good.

Show Illustration #18

If someone says that to you, show him what God says. According to God's Word, even the right things a person does before he believes in the Saviour, are as filthy, dirty rags to God. (See Isaiah 64:6; compare Psalm 14:2-3.) Explain that because of God's great love, He gave His precious Son to take the punishment we deserve. By dying on the cross, the Lord Jesus has done all He can to buy each one back for Himself. Ask your friend if he is willing to place his trust in Christ.

This is one way you can serve the Lord. There are others. (*Teacher:* Have students mention exactly what can be done for God this day, this week. Have them list these in their notebooks.)

We don't serve our Lord and Master with fear as the slaves did. We don't serve Him because we have to. We serve Him gladly because we love Him. And we love Him because He loved us first. (See 1 John 4:19.)

www.ingramcontent.com/pod-product-compliance
Lightning Source LLC
Chambersburg PA
CBHW060802090426
42736CB00002B/121